# In Memoriam: Casgliad O Donau Y Diweddar John Roberts,henllan

## John Roberts

Yr eiddoch yn gywir
John Roberts.

# In Memoriam.

# CASGLIAD O DONAU

### Y DIWEDDAR

## JOHN ROBERTS,

### HENLLAN.

## YNGHYDA RHAGDRAETH AC ATTODIAD:

### DAN OLYGIAETH

## W. H. ROBERTS.

LLUNDAIN:
ARGRAPHWYD DROS Y CYHOEDDWR
GAN
J. HADDON & CO., 3, BOUVERIE STREET, FLEET STREET.
1876.

TO

THE CHERISHED AND HONOURED

Memory

OF

A FATHER,

WHO, WHILE ON EARTH,

TRIED TO DO HIS DUTY IN HIS DAY AND GENERATION,

AND NOW

IS ENTERED INTO THE JOY OF HIS LORD,

THIS LITTLE BOOK

Is Affectionately Dedicated

BY

HIS SONS.

# RHAGYMADRODD.

SYN, mae yn bosibl, fydd gan lawer ddeall fod holl gynnyr-chion fy nhad yn gynnwysedig yn y gyfrol hon, ac nad oes dim cyfansoddiad o'i waith o nodwedd fwy ymhongar na'r salm-don, neu y don gynulleidfaol. Ond dyna y ffaith. Er treulio o hono oes weithgar o bump a deugain o flynyddoedd a rhagor gyda cherddoriaeth, nid ysgrifenodd ddim dros ben yr hyn a geir yma. Ymddengys iddo ymroi yn hollol ymron i gasglu hen donau rhag myned ar gyfrgoll, ac i addasu at wasa-naeth y cyssegr y cyfryw o honynt ag a dybiai yn deilwng o hyny. Hyn, ar fyr eiriau, gyda dal i fyny yn wastad y lle mawr a berthynai i fawl yn yr addoliad dwyfol, a'r pwysigrwydd o'i fod yn weddaidd a dyrchafedig, ydyw hanes ei yrfa gerddorol.

Afreidiol dweyd o honof ddim am y tonau. Gwelir oddiwrth fy ngwaith yn eu cyhoeddi beth yw fy marn i am eu teilyngdod. Barn cariad, o bosibl, a roddaf fi arnynt, a barn nas gallaf ddysgwyl eraill i'w chyfranogi gyda mi, o leiaf i'r un graddau. Ond pa dyb bynag a goleddir am eu teilyngdod cynwynol, tybied yr wyf nad oes neb a warafun iddynt rywfaint o werth hanesyddol, yn gymaint a'u bod yn gyfansoddiadau gwr a wnaeth ei ran tuagat ddwyn i mewn gyfnod newydd, a chyfnod rhagorach yn hanes cerddoriaeth gyssegredig ei wlad.

Dymunaf gydnabod y ddyled fawr o ddiolchgarwch sydd arnaf i un o hen gyfeillion fy nhad am ei Ragdraeth, ac am y tonau y mae y llythyrenau W. J. H. yn nglyn â hwynt: i'r cyfeillion ereill a'm hanrhegasant â chyfieithiadau, &c., o emynau; ac, yn arbenig, i'r derbynwyr hynaws, am eu cefnogaeth dirion, heb yr hon nis gallaswn gyflawni yr hyn sydd wedi bod yn ddymuniad calon genyf ers llawer dydd.

W. H. ROBERTS.

SEACOMBE,
*Mai 12fed, 1876.*

# INTRODUCTION.

A FEW prefatory remarks on Welsh Psalmody will not be deemed inappropriate as a prelude to the present little collection of a veteran Welsh musician's original tunes, most of which now appear for the first time.

The materials for a well-authenticated history of the subject are scanty. Most that we know is based upon tradition, more or less vague. Metrical Psalmody in the vernacular tongue was, as is well known, established in these islands after the Reformation. When it first took root in Wales is uncertain, but many of the native melodies bear indications that Gregorian music must have flourished in the various monastic institutions which then overspread the principality, and that its peculiar scales must have laid too strong a hold upon the national ear to be easily forgotten. Traces of its influence may still be discovered in many of our older Welsh tunes, and notably in what is familiarly known as the "*hwyl*" in popular Welsh preaching. For any authentic account of the condition of Church Music in Wales until the "Revival," the materials are very scanty. The country parish clerk was of course musical *ex officio;* and as his ecclesiastical superiors then deemed singing a thing to be turned over to him and his artisan associates, he had it all his own way. He often composed the music, such as it was, himself, and assumed to direct its performance. On great occasions an anthem, such as "*A bydd arwyddion*," was performed, the effect of which would appear strange to us now. He collected a perfect Nebuchadnezzar's band around him for the display—clarionet, flute, bassoon, violin, violoncello; and of course all the performers were equally learned. It was a sort of musical *Commune*, in which none aspired to lead, none condescended to follow. At it they went indiscriminately, and those who got first to the end of the composition struck in at the point where the majority of the rest happened to have arrived; so that if they proceeded a little wildly on their way, they generally contrived to end in unison.* The congregation meanwhile listened with interest, but stood mute : such fine music was too difficult for their humble ears. These, however, were the evil days of pluralities and non-resident benefice-holders ; and it need scarcely be said that musical matters wear a very different aspect in the Welsh Established Church now-a-days, congregational psalmody being cultivated with earnestness, assiduity, and success.

Among the Nonconformists, in the latter decades of the last century, the more emotional hymns of Williams of Pantycelyn had superseded in popular favour the sameness and frigidity of Archdeacon Prys' metrical psalms. Hymn-singing, distinctly congregational, had now become an in-

---

* Matters were not much better in England at the time. A typical specimen of the old-fashioned parish clerk, drawn by the master-hand of " George Eliot," grumbles to his rector thus :—" I have lived in the village, man and boy, sixty year come St. Thomas, and collected th' Easter dues for Mr. Blick before your reverence come into the parish, and been at the ringin' o' every bell and the diggin' o' every grave, *and sung i' the quire long afore Bartle Massey come from nobody knows where, wi' his counter-singing and fine anthems as puts everybody out but himself, one takin' it up after another like sheep a-bleatin' i' th' fold.*"—ADAM BEDE, p. 47.

Again, the performance of a representative village choir is thus described :—" As the moment of psalmody approached, by some process to me as mysterious and untraceable as the opening of the flowers or the breaking out of the stars, a slate appeared in front of the gallery, advertising in bold characters the psalm about to be sung, lest the sonorous announcement of the clerk should still leave the bucolic mind in doubt on that head. Then followed the migration of the clerk to the gallery, where, in company with a bassoon, two key-bugles, a carpenter—understood to have an amazing power of singing ' counter,'—and two lesser musical stars, he formed the complement of a choir, regarded in Shepperton as one of distinguished attraction, occasionally known to draw hearers from the next parish. The innovation of hymn-books was as yet undreamed of ; even the ' New Version ' was regarded with a sort of melancholy tolerance, as part of the common degeneracy in a time when prices had dwindled, and a cotton gown was no longer stout enough to last a life-time ; for the lyrical taste of the best heads in Shepperton had been formed on Sternhold and Hopkins. But the greatest triumphs of the Shepperton choir were reserved for the Sundays when the slate announced an ANTHEM, with a dignified abstinence from particularisation, both words and music lying far beyond the reach of the most ambitious amateur in the congregation :—an anthem in which the key-bugles always ran away at a great pace, while the bassoon every now and then boomed a flying shot after them."—SCENES OF CLERICAL LIFE, pp. 4, 5.

·tegral part of their service, just as the singing of the metrical psalms of Marot by the followers of Calvin, at Geneva, came to constitute the admitted badge of Protestantism. There could have been few tunes ready-made to suit the numerous new metres then introduced (8.7.3, 8.7.4, 7.6, &c., &c.), and a number of melodies were produced by different "blaenoriaid canu" (men gifted with "awen," but musically illiterate), and, being learnt by the enormous crowds which used to attend the various religious gatherings, were disseminated orally throughout the principality. Some of these melodies are unmistakably original, others appear to bear internal evidence of being unconsciously based upon floating reminiscences of the Gregorian airs used in the various monastic institutions which studded the land previous to the dissolution of the monasteries. However that may be, a large proportion of these tunes possess musical merit of a high order. They must have been sung in unison generally, or at all events with an extemporised bass and tenor, which would scarcely bear inspection these days, when a scientific knowledge of harmony is so widely diffused. It is to Mr. John Roberts of Henllan that the credit attaches of having presented for the first time a large proportion of these traditional tunes in a practicable form to his fellow-countrymen, clothed in simple yet pure and appropriate harmony. They were included in a collection entitled "Caniadau y Cyssegr," published at Denbigh in 1839. His arrangements therein, while making little pretence to pedantic elaboration, are marked by a degree of accuracy to which many of his successors in the same field can hardly lay claim. The publication of that book was particularly opportune, as the country was at the time beginning to be inundated with a deluge of vulgar twaddle by Clark of Canterbury, Purday, Jarman, *et hoc genus omne*, which bade fair to ruin a purer taste in psalmody. It effectually stemmed the tide and torrent of this sing-song nonsense, and the beneficial effects of his labours are still manifest in the taste displayed in the better of our collections of tunes to the present day. Most of the tunes included in that collection (now out of print) are plain, straightforward chorales—musical servants-of-all-work, so to speak—which will serve for any words of sentiment corresponding to the mode in which the music is written. A proportion, however (Edifeiriol, &c.), against whom a regular crusade has been preached by musical purists, were adapted to special hymns. Of course this principle of exclusive adaptation, like many others, may be overdone, but in moderation it may perhaps be pronounced sound. It is maintained, and with no little truth, in Germany, that church-music should be as much associated with the words in people's minds as secular music—" *Hen wlad fy Nhadau* " for instance—is with the songs to which it is adapted. A familiar example in point is the case of the Lutheran chorales of that country, such as " *Eine feste burg.*" The hymn and its appropriate tune are designed to go together : the tune to suggest the words of the hymn, the hymn to call up the memory of the tune : the hymn to impart a sentiment to the tune, and, in turn, to catch an impression from it.

In noting down the melodies from the singing of different persons, Mr. Roberts appears to have jotted them down *notatim* as they were sung—passing notes and all. Of late, at any rate since the publication of Mr. Havergal's Preface to his " Old Church Psalmody," it has been the fashion to decry this exact transcription; old melodies having been by some " arrangers " stripped of what unpretending little graces they had, and all but spoilt. Now it is open to question, whether this process of high-handed pruning is exactly justifiable ; at any rate, if it is to be done at all, it should be done by a master. In inferior hands it amounts simply to evisceration, and the melody is left a dry husk. If those who prefer to leave traditional melodies in their original form have erred, at all events they have erred in good company—that of John Sebastian Bach, whom few will accuse of being short of learning or classical taste; see, for instance, Nos. 13, 45, 71, 84, 111, 182 in his *Choralgesangebuch* (Leipsic edition, by Becker, 1831).

The present little book consists mainly of a selection of Mr. Roberts' own compositions, characterised by good taste throughout, simple in style, but melodious, and effectively harmonised. I make little doubt they will be found a welcome addition to the repertory of many a choir.

W. J. H.

---

Since the above was written, Mr. Roberts quietly breathed his last on the 4th of April, 1876, in the 70th age of his age.

  •    •    •    •    •    •    •    •

" Thou wilt keep him in perfect peace, whose mind is stayed on Thee ; because he trusteth in Thee."

# TONAU

## Y DIWEDDAR

# JOHN ROBERTS.

# Abermeirig. M. S.

( 2 )

## SALM XLV.

1 CLYW hyn, O ferch! a hefyd gwel,
  Ac â chlust isel gwrando :
Mae 'n rhaid it' ollwng pawb o'th wlad,
  A thŷ dy dad yn angho'.

2 Yna bydd gan y Brenin wych
  Gael edrych ar dy degwch :
Dy Arglwydd yw, gwna iddo foes,
  I gael i'th oes hyfrydwch.

3 Ond merch y Brenin glân o fewn,
  Anrhydedd llawn sydd iddi ;
A gwisg o aur a gemau glân,
  Oddi allan sydd am dani.

E. PRYS.

## SALM XLVIII.

EWCH, ewch oddi amgylch Seion sail,
  A'i thyrau adail rhifwch ;
Ei chadarn fur, a'i phlasau draw,
  I'r oes a ddaw mynegwch.

E. PRYS.

## PSALM XXIII.

1 THE King of love my Shepherd is,
  Whose goodness faileth never ;
I nothing lack if I am His
  And He is mine for ever.

2 And so through all the length of days
  Thy goodness faileth never ;
Good Shepherd, may I sing thy praise
  Within Thy house for ever.

ANON.

# Aberystwyth. 7au., 6 ll.

1840.

1 HYFRYD lais efengyl hedd,
   Sydd yn galw pawb i'r wledd:
Mae gwahoddiad llawn at Grist—
Oes, i'r tlawd, newynog, trist:
Pob cyflawnder ynddo gewch—
Dewch a chroesaw, dlodion, dewch.

2 Iesu gaiff y clod i gyd;
   Ymaith dug bechodau 'r byd:
Rhoes Ei Hunan yn ein lle—
Bellach, beth na rydd Efe?
Haleluia, llawenhewch—
Dewch, moliennwch, byth na thewch.

PEDR FARDD.

1 CHRIST, Whose glory fills the skies,
   Christ, the true, the only light,
Sun of righteousness, arise,
   Triumph o'er the shades of night!
Day-spring from on high, be near!
Day-star, in my heart appear!

2 Dark and cheerless is the morn
   Unaccompanied by Thee;
Joyless is the day's return,
   Till Thy mercy's beams I see;
Till they inward light impart,
Glad my eyes, and warm my heart.

3 Visit then this soul of mine,
   Pierce the gloom of sin and grief!
Fill me, Radiancy Divine,
   Scatter all my unbelief!
More and more Thyself display,
Shining to the perfect day!

C. WESLEY.

( 5 )

# Capel Dewi. 8.7.D.

1842.

( 6 )

1 MÔR sydd ynot o fendithion,
   Heb waelodion iddo 'n bod ;
Y mae 'n llanw 'mlaen bob mynyd ;
   Nid oes diwedd ar Dy glod :
Dy enw beunydd sy'n ymdaenu
   Fel goleuni bore wawr ;
Bydd telynau 'n canu iddo,
   Fel rhifedi gwellt y llawr.

2 Nis gall holl hyfrydwch natur,
   A'i melysdra pena' i maes,
Fyth gymharu â lleferydd
   Hyfryd pur, maddeuol ras :
Gâd im' glywed sŵn Dy eiriau—
   Awdurdodol eiriau 'r nef—
Oddi mewn yn creu hyfrydwch,
   Nad oes mo'i gyffelyb ef.

WILLIAMS.

1 SWEET the moments, rich in blessing,
   Which before the cross we spend,
Life, and health, and peace possessing,
   From the sinner's dying Friend :
Here we rest, in wonder viewing
   All our sins on Jesus laid,
Here we see redemption flowing
   From the sacrifice He made.

2 Here we find the dawn of heaven,
   While upon the cross we gaze,
See our trespasses forgiven,
   And our songs of triumph raise :
Oh ! that near the cross abiding,
   We may to the Saviour cleave,
Nought with Him our hearts dividing,
   All for Him content to leave.

ALLEN.

( 7 )

B

# Dirgelwch. M.H.

1 HENFFYCH i enw Iesu gwiw!
   Syrthiwch o'i flaen, angylion Duw;
Rhowch iddo barch, holl deulu'r nef—
Yn Arglwydd pawb, coronwch Ef.

2 Doed y cenhedloedd o bob iaith,
Trwy holl derfynau'r ddaear faith,
I ganu'n llafar iawn eu llef—
Yn Arglwydd pawb, coronwch Ef.

3 O! na chaem gyda'r nefol lu,
Syrthio wrth draed ein Harglwydd fry;
Ac uno'n llon a hwy ein llef—
Yn Arglwydd pawb, coronwch Ef.
              *O Gasgliad y Parch.* R. PHILLIPS.


1 SWEET is the work, my God, my King,
   To praise Thy name, give thanks and sing;
To show Thy love by morning light,
   And talk of all Thy truth at night.

2 Sweet is the day of sacred rest,
   No mortal cares shall seize my breast;
Oh, may my heart in tune be found,
   Like David's harp of solemn sound.
                 WATTS.

( 9 )

# Eifion. 7.6. D.

1839.

( 10 )

1 ANGELION doent yn gysson,
   Rifedi gwlith y wawr,
Rhoent eu coronau euraidd
   O flaen y fainc i lawr :
Chwareuant eu telynau,
   Yn nghyd â'r saint yn un—
Fyth, fyth, ni chanant ddigon
   Am Dduwdod yn y dyn.

2 O! foroedd o ddoethineb
   Oedd yn y Duwdod mawr
Pan y cyfranai 'i gariad
   I bryfed gwael y llawr ;
A gwneuthur i'w drugaredd,
   Â'i dostur maith yn nghyd,
I redeg megys afon
   Lifeiriol dros y byd !

                    WILLIAMS.


## PSALM LXXII.

1 HAIL to the Lord's Anointed !
   Great David's greater Son ;
Hail, in the time appointed,
   His reign on earth begun !
He comes to break oppression,
   To set the captive free ;
To take away transgression,
   And rule in equity.

2 O'er every foe victorious,
   He on His throne shall rest ;
From age to age more glorious,
   All blessing, and all blest.
The tide of time shall never
   His covenant remove ;
His name shall stand for ever ;
   His great, best name of Love !

                    MONTGOMERY.

# Escol. 7.6.5.

1838.

( 12 )

1 FRY yn Nghaersalem dawel,
  Yn mhell o swn y rhyfel,
    Caf uchel ganu clod ;
  Fy nefoedd ddi-boen,
  Fydd gweled yr Oen—
    Fe dderfydd son am bechod.

2 Mi gysgaf hûn yn dawel
  Dros ennyd yn y grafel
    Nes dattod trefn y rhod ;
  Ac yna mewn hedd,
  Y codaf o'm bedd,
    Ar ddysglaer wedd fy Mhriod.

MORGAN RHYS.

1 IN Jesus sweetly sleeping,
  Safe in His tender keeping,
    We in the grave shall rest ;
  And when we awake
  Our flight we shall take
    To realms that know no weeping.

2 There shall we dwell for ever,
  And nought our hearts shall sever
    From peace, and joy, and rest ;
  No sorrow, or sin,
  Shall enter within
    The mansions of our Saviour.

3 With love and admiration,
  With praise and adoration,
    Our eyes shall dwell on Him ;
  His grace we shall sing,
  Heaven's courts shall all ring,
    In praise for His salvation.

REV. JOHN ROBERTS,
Edinburgh.

## Gilead. 8.7.3.

1839.

( 14 )

1 DEUWCH hil syrthiedig Adda,
    Daeth y Jubil fawr o hedd ;
Galwad sydd ar bawb o'r enw,
    I fwynhau tragwyddol wledd :
Bwrdd yn llawn, yma gawn,
O foreuddydd hyd brydnawn.

2 Ceisiwch wisgoedd y briodas—
    Gwisgoedd hyfryd hardd eu lliw ;
Nid oes enw teilwng arnynt,
    Ond cyfiawnder pur fy Nuw :
Llian main ydyw rhai 'n,
Sydd yn cuddio pob rhyw staen.

3 Dyma wledd y cewch ddanteithion,
    Yma cewch faddeuant rhad ;
Yma cewch chwi brofi cariad—
    Hedd yn nofio yn y gwaed :
Dowch yn awr, dyrfa fawr,
Ac eisteddwch yma i lawr.

                          WILLIAMS.


1 COME to Calvary's holy mountain,
    Sinners ruined by the fall ;
Here a pure and healing fountain
    Flows to you, to me, to all,
In a full, perpetual tide,
Opened when our Saviour died.

2 Come in sorrow and contrition,
    Wounded, impotent, and blind ;
Here the guilty, free remission,
    Here the troubled, peace may find :
Health this fountain will restore,
He that drinks shall thirst no more.

                          MONTGOMERY.

# Goppa. 8.3.6.

1874.

1 AM fendithion y goleuni,
    Clod i'm Duw,
    Heno'n wiw,
Rhyfedd yw'th ddaioni.

2 Dan Dy gysgod heno'n dawel,
    Llechu wnaf,
    Gyda'm Naf
Byddaf yn ddiogel.

3 Ac os hon fydd nos fy angeu,
    Iesu cu,
    Derbyn Di
F'yspryd i Dy freichiau.

                    MORRIS DAVIES.


1 JESU, let Thy sufferings ease us ;
    Saviour, Lord,
    Speak the word,
By Thy death, release us.

2 Hear us, Lord, our sins confessing ;
    O relieve ;
    Saviour give,
Give us now Thy blessing.

3 Save us now, and still deliver ;
    Cast out sin,
    Enter in,
Keep Thine house for ever.

                    J. WESLEY.

# Gwalchmai. M.C.

1850.

1 MAE 'n hyfryd meddwl ambell dro,
    Wrth deithio anial le,
  Ar ol ein holl flinderau dwys,
    Cawn orphwys yn y ne'.

2 Pan ar ddiffygio gan y daith.
    A lludded maith y lle,
  Mor hoff yw gwybod—wedi hyn,
    Cawn orphwys yn y ne'.

3 Er colli ein cyfeillion hoff,
    Yn yr Iorddonen gref,
  Mae 'n felus meddwl—eto 'nghyd,
    Cawn gwrddyd yn y nef.
                IEUAN GLAN GEIRIONYDD.


1 WHEN I can read my title clear
    To mansions in the skies,
  I bid farewell to every fear,
    And wipe my weeping eyes.

2 Let cares like a wild deluge come,
    And storms of sorrow fall,
  May I but safely reach my home,
    My God, my heaven, my all.

3 There shall I bathe my weary soul
    In seas of heavenly rest,
  And not a wave of trouble roll
    Across my peaceful breast.
                        WATTS.

# Gwalia. 10. 11.

1838.

1    RHYW afon a gaed,
      O ddwfr ac o waed—
O'r orsedd ddysgleirdeg, mae 'n rhedeg yn rhad;
    I wella fy mriw,
    Fy meiau o bob rhyw,
'A chànu fy enaid, er dued ei liw.

2    Boed yma fy nyth,
    A'm bywyd i byth—
Yn nghlwyfau 'r Oen tyner, a'i lawnder di-lyth;
    Ac yna caf fyw,
    Er croesau o bob rhyw,
A'm henaid yn llawen dan aden fy Nuw.

                  WILLIAMS.


## PSALM CIV.

1    O WORSHIP the King
      All glorious above,
O gratefully sing His power and His love;
    Our Shield and Defender,
    The Ancient of days,
Pavilioned in splendour, and girded with praise.

2    Frail children of dust,
    And feeble as frail,
In Thee do we trust, nor find Thee to fail.
    Thy mercies how tender!
    How firm to the end!
Our Maker, Defender, Redeemer, and Friend.

              SIR R. GRANT.

# Iachawdwriaeth. 8.7.D.

1829.

1 O! FY Iesu! 'Mhriod anwyl!
   Cofia eiddil gwael di-lun,
Sydd yn gwywo bob mynydyn,
   Sydd yn blino arno 'i hun :
Tro fy ngolwg at Dy haeddiant,
   A'th drugaredd ryfedd rad ;
Rho dangnefedd yn fy mynwes,
   Rho faddeuant yn Dy waed.

2 Anfon un pelydryn tirion,
   O Dy orsedd ddysglaer fry,
Nes bo 'r dydd yn siriol wenu,
   Ar ol noswaith dywell ddu ;
A fy enaid yn cael myned,
   Fel aderyn uwch y llawr,
Ar adenydd cariad cynhes,
   I Dy fynwes, Iesu mawr !

*Y Parch.* D. CHARLES, IEU.


1 JESUS, for Thy love most tender,
   On the cross for sinners shown,
We would praise Thee, and surrender
   All our hearts to be Thine own :
With so blest a Friend provided,
   We upon our way would go,
Sure of being safely guided,
   Guarded well from every foe.

2 Every day will be the brighter,
   When Thy gracious face we see ;
Every burden will be lighter,
   When we know it comes from Thee :
Spread Thy love's broad banner o'er us,
   Give us strength to serve and wait,
Till Thy glory breaks before us,
   Through the city's open gate.

J. D. BURNS.

( 23 )

C

# Kyrie Eleison.

*Ar ol y degfed gorchymyn.*

ARGLWYDD, trugarha wrthym, a gostwng ein calonau i gadw'r gyfraith hon.


*Ar ol y degfed gorchymyn.*

ARGLWYDD, trugarha wrthym, ac ysgrifena'r holl ddeddfau hyn yn ein calonau, ni a atolygwn i Ti.

# Llanddowror. M.S.

( 26 )

## SALM LXXXVII.

1 O DDINAS Duw, preswylfa'r Ion,
    Mawr ydyw'r son am danad :
  A gogoneddus air it' sydd
    Goruwch trigfëydd yr holl wlad.

2 Dywedir hyn am Seion bêr,
    Fe anwyd llawer ynddi
  Nid ambell un : can's swccwr da
    Yw Duw goruchaf iddi.

3 Pob cantor tafod, cerddor tant,
    I Ti y canant fawrglod :
  A thrwy lawenydd mae'n parhau
    Fy holl ffynonau ynod.

E. PRYS.

## PSALM CXXXVI.

1 G IVE thanks to God, for good is He ;
    For mercy hath He ever :
  Thanks to the God of gods give ye ;
    For His grace faileth never.

2 Thanks give the Lord of lords unto ;
    For mercy hath He ever :
  Who only wonders great can do ;
    For His grace faileth never.

*Scottish Version.*

## Llanwenog. 8.7.3.

1839.

( 28 )

1 DACW'R ffynon wedi ei hagor,
　　A ddysgwyliwyd lawer oes;
'Nawr yn llifo fel y grisial
　　Pur o'i ystlys ar y groes :
Dwr a gwaed, rydd iachâd,
I'r pechadur mwya' gaed.

2 Dacw'r hoelion geirwon llymion,
　　Wedi eu curo 'nawr i dre' ;
Dacw'r bicell yn trywanu
　　I mewn o dan ei ystlys E' :
Dacw boen, addfwyn Oen,
Yn rhoi'r nefoedd dewi son.

WILLIAMS.


1 SEE the Saviour bleeding, dying,
　　On the cross, in pain and shame !
On His death alone relying,
　　Would I now Thy mercy claim :
Oh ! let me, Lord, by Thee,
Now in Him accepted be.

2 In the great Propitiation
　　Made upon th' accursèd tree,
There is hope of full salvation,
　　Pardon, peace, and joy, for me :
Jesus' blood, once that flowed,
Is my all and all with God.

REV. JOHN ROBERTS,
*Edinburgh.*

( 29 )

# Meifod. M.S.

1 O! BRYSIA, Arglwydd, clyw fy llais—
  O brysur gelwais arnat;
O'r man lle b'wyf, gwrando fy llef,
  A doed i'r nef hyd atat.

2 O Arglwydd! gosod, rhag gair ffraeth,
  Gadwraeth ar fy ngenau;
Rhag im' gamdd'wedyd, gosod ddôr
  Ar gyfor fy ngwefusau.

3 Mae 'ngolwg a'm holl obaith i,
  Duw! arnat Ti dy hunan:
O! bydd Di 'n unig yn fy mhlaid,
  Na fwrw f' enaid allan.

E. PRYS.


1 WITH trembling heart and blushing face,
  I seek Thy grace, O Saviour!
Vile and unworthy though I be,
  Oh! grant to me Thy favour.

2 All my transgressions, Lord, forgive,
  Oh! let me live before Thee;
Save me, and I Thy name will praise,
  And all my days adore Thee.

REV. JOHN ROBERTS,
*Edinburgh.*

# Nefol Afon. 9.8.

1859.

( 32 )

1 O! ARWAIN fy enaid i'r dyfroedd—
   Y dyfroedd sy'n afon mor bur;
Y dyfroedd a dorant fy syched,
   Er trymed fy nolur a'm cur:
Y dyfroedd tragwyddol eu tarddiad,
   Y dyfroedd sy heb waelod na thrai;
Y dyfroedd a olchant fy enaid,
   Er dued, er amled fy mai.

2 Da iawn i bechadur fod afon
   A ylch yr aflanaf yn wyn;
Hi darddodd o'r nefoedd yn gysson
   Hi ffrydiodd ar Galfari fryn:
Hi lifodd i'r anial cenedlig,
   Hi olchodd fil miloedd yn lân;
Hi ylch ei miliynau 'n llwyr ganaid,
   Cyn rhoddi llawr daiar ar dân.

                    T. JONES, *Dinbych.*


1 OH! lead where the life-giving waters
   In fathomless purity flow,
From fountains eternal in heaven
   To gladden this desert below;
Where sin-stricken pilgrims for ever
   Their feverish thirst may allay,
Where floods of His love and His mercy
   Wash guilt and uncleanness away.

2 Oh! founts of compassion still springing
   From the rocks of His justice above,
Oh! torrent from Calvary, pouring
   The wealth of His pity and love,
Flow onward still deeper and wider,
   Through desert and wilderness drear,
The steps of the pilgrims to strengthen,
   The desolate spirit to cheer.

                    *Trans. by* D. R. C.

# Nefydd. 6.8.

1  ER myned oll yn gaeth,
      A chyfeiliorni'n mhell,
   Trwy Iesu Grist fe ddaeth
      In' etifeddiaeth well:
   Gwnaeth iawn i'w Dad, a hedd i ni,
   Trwy waed Ei groes ar Galfari.

2  Aed sain efengyl gras
      O gwmpas daear lawr:
   Doed pawb i brofi blas
      Yr iachawdwriaeth fawr:
   I Seion wiw doed torf ddi-ri',
   Wrth sain per udgorn Jubili.

                        PEDR FARDD.


1  JOIN all the glorious names
      Of wisdom, love, and power,
   That ever mortals knew,
      That angels ever bore:
   All are too mean to speak His worth,
   Too mean to set my Saviour forth.

2  My Saviour and my Lord,
      My Conqueror and my King,
   Thy sceptre and Thy sword,
      Thy reigning grace I sing:
   Thine is the power; behold, I sit
   In willing bonds before Thy feet.

                        WATTS.

## Offrwm Moliant. 8.7.4.

1850.

1 PECHOD yma, cariad acw,
   Fu yno yn y glorian fawr;
Ac er trymed oedd y pechod,
   Cariad bwysodd hyd y llawr:
      Gair " Gorphenwyd,"
Wnaeth i'r glorian bwysig droi.

2 Dacw gariad, dacw bechod
   Heddyw'u dau ar ben y bryn;
Hwn sy'n gryf, hwn acw'n gadarn,
   Pwy ennilla'r ymgyrch hyn?
      Cariad, cariad
Welai'n perffaith gario'r dydd.

WILLIAMS.

1 'TWAS Thy love, O God, that knew us
   Earth's foundations long before;
That same love to Jesus drew us,
   By its sweet, constraining power,
      And will keep us
Safely, now and evermore.

2 God of love, our souls adore Thee!
   We would still Thy grace proclaim,
Till we cast our crowns before Thee,
   And in glory praise Thy name:
      Hallelujah!
Be to God and to the Lamb.

DECK.

( 37 )

## Pantycelyn. M.C.

1 MAE brodyr imi aeth yn mlaen,
  Yn holliach a chytûn ;
  Deng mil o filoedd yw eu cân,
  Er hyn, nid yw ond un.

2 Mae pawb o'r brodyr yno 'n un,
  Heb neb yn tynu 'n groes,
  Yn moli 'r Duwdod yn y Dyn,
  A chofio angeu loes.

3 Ni theimlir yno unrhyw boen,
  Na chwyno gan un clwy',
  Ond pawb mewn hwyl yn moli 'r Oen,
  I dragwyddoldeb mwy.
                              D. MORUS.


1 COME, let us join our cheerful songs
  With angels round the throne,
  Ten thousand thousand are their tongues,
  But all their joys are one.

2 Jesus is worthy to receive
  Honour and power divine ;
  And blessings more than we can give,
  Be, Lord, for ever Thine.

3 The whole creation join in one
  To bless the sacred name
  Of Him that sits upon the throne,
  And to adore the Lamb.
                              WATTS.

# Prestatyn. M.S.

1863.

1 NA foed i'm henaid euog, trist,
     Ond haeddiant Crist yn gyfran ;
  Ei aberth Ef, llawn ddigon yw
     I feddwl Duw ei hunan.

2 Rhyfeddir byth y geni 'n dlawd,
     Y byw dan wawd a chroesau,
  Y dyoddef cosp heb unrhyw fai,
     A'r ufuddhau heb rwymau.

3 Yr uchel gân fydd, " Iddo Ef,"
     Trwy nef y nef yn seinio ;
  Yr ing, yr Iawn, a'r gwaedlyd chwys,
     A felus gofir yno.
                    ERYRON GWYLLT WALIA.


## PSALM XXXIV.

1 EXTOL the Lord with me, let us
     Exalt His name together ;
  I sought the Lord, He heard, and did
     Me from all fears deliver.

2 They looked to Him and lightened were,
     Not shamèd were their faces ;
  This poor man cried, God heard and saved
     Him from all his distresses.
                    *Scottish Version.*

# Rhyd y bedd. 8.7., 4 ll,

1839.

( 42 )

1 O! IACHAWDWR pechaduriaid,
    Sydd a'r gallu yn Dy law,
  Rho oleuni, hwylia'm henaid
    Dros y cefnfor garw draw.

2 Gad i'r wawr fod o fy wyneb,
    Rho fy enaid llesg yn rhydd ;
  Nes i'r haulwen ddysglaer godi,
    Tywys fi wrth y seren ddydd.

WILLIAMS.

1 GENTLY, Lord, O gently lead us,
    Through this gloomy vale of tears,
  Through the changes Thou'st decreed us,
    Till our last great change appears.

2 In the hour of pains and anguish,
    In the hour when death is near,
  Suffer not our hearts to languish,
    Suffer not our souls to fear.

3 When this mortal life is ended,
    Bid us in Thine arms to rest,
  Till, by angel-bands attended,
    We awake among the blest.

HASTINGS.

# Aled. 6.5.

W. J. R.

FINE.

( 46 )

1 AR lan Iorddonen ddofn
   'R wy'n oedi 'n nychlyd,
Mewn blys myn'd trwy—ac ofn
   Ei stormydd enbyd ;
O! na b'ai modd i mi
Ysgoi ei hymchwydd hi,
A hedfan uwch ei lli'
   I'r Ganaan hyfryd !

2 Wrth gofio grym y dwr,
   A'i thonog genlli',
A'r mynych rymus wr
   A suddodd ynddi—
Mae braw ar f'enaid gwan
Mai boddi fydd fy rhan,
Cyn cyrhaedd tawel lan
   Bro y goleuni.

3 Ond pan y gwelwyf draw
   Ar fynydd Seion,
Yn iach, heb boen na braw,
   Fy hen gyfeillion—
Pa ham yr ofnaf mwy ?
Y Duw a'u daliodd hwy,
A'm dyga innau drwy
   Ei dyfroedd dyfnion.
            IEUAN GLAN GEIRIONYDD.


1 O LORD, give me Thy hand,
   When I, poor mortal,
With fear and trembling stand,
   At Death's dark portal ;
Its gloom shall not dismay,
Its night shall be as day,
If Thou but lead the way
   To life immortal.
            H. Ll. J.

## Arabia. 8au, 8 ll.

W. J. WHITE.
Cynghaneddwyd gan W. J. H.

( 48 )

MI wn fod fy Mhrynwr yn fyw,
  A'm prynodd â thaliad mor ddrud,
Fe saif ar y ddaear, gwir yw,
  Yn niwedd holl oesoedd y byd :
Er ised a gwaeled fy ngwedd,
  Teyrnasu mae Mhrynwr a 'Mrawd ;
Ac er fy malurio'n y bedd,
  Ei weled gaf eto'n fy nghnawd.

                    T. JONES, *Dinbych.*


1 INSPIRER and Hearer of prayer,
  Thou Shepherd, and Guardian of Thine,
My all to Thy covenant care
  I, sleeping and waking, resign.
Thy ministering spirits descend
  To watch, while Thy saints are asleep ;
By day and by night they attend,
  The heirs of salvation to keep.


2 Thy worship no interval knows,
  Their fervour is still on the wing ;
And, while they protect my repose,
  They chant to the praise of my King :
I, too, at the season ordained
  Their chorus for ever shall join ;
And love, and adore, without end,
  Their faithful Creator, and mine.

# Bosnia. 8.6.5.

Y diweddar Barch.
J. B. DYKES, M.A., Mus. Doc.

( 50 )

1 DADSEINIWN orfoleddus glod
   Ein Prynwr, Duw a dyn ;
Gwaredwr yw Ef, Ei fraich sydd yn gref,
   Dioddefodd ein haeddiant Ei Hun.

2 Ei gnawd, a ddrylliwyd ar y pren,
   Yw bara 'n henaid byw ;
Ei waed yw y gwin sy'n lloni pob un,
   Ein helaeth gynnaliaeth ni yw.

3 Coffawn am angau trist y groes
   Gyda diolchus ffydd :
Cyfiawnder ga'dd iawn, y taljad oedd lawn,
   Rhoed ninnau, ddyledwyr, yn rhydd.

                       MORRIS DAVIES.


1 COME, let us raise triumphant praise
   To Jesus, God and man :
Who died that even we from death might be free ;
   Who loved us or e'er time began.

2 His body broken on the cross,
   Is now our souls' true bread ;
His blood maketh glad the faint and the sad,
   The guiltiest in Him hath no dread.

3 Grant us, O God, with fearful joy
   To make remembrance meet !
And of Thy great grace reveal Jesu's face,
   Ineffably glorious and sweet.

          *Trans. by* REV. ELLIS EDWARDS, M.A.

# Caerphili. 7.3.

Alaw Gymreig.
Cynghaneddwyd gan W. J. H.

( 52 )

1 AETH llu o'r genedl gyfion,
    Oll yn iach, oll yn iach;
I santaidd ddinas Seion,
    Oll yn iach;
Mae eto dyrfa yn dyfod,
O'r cystudd mawr a'r trallod,
Cawn yno gyd-gyfarfod,
  Oll yn iach, oll yn iach;
Ar ddysglaer wedd ein Priod,
    Oll yn iach.

*O " Grawnsypiau Canaan."*

1 O sinner, full of sorrow,
    Come to Me, come to Me;
Why wait until the morrow?
    Come to Me.
For thee I am sadly sighing,
To save thee ever trying,
To thee I am always crying
  Come to Me, come to Me;
For thee I am daily dying;
    Come to Me.

2 By these My wounds I claim thee,
    Come to Me, come to Me;
And coming who shall blame thee?
    Come to Me.
O Lord, my heart is burning,
For Thee my soul is yearning,
My feet, Thy way discerning,
  Turn to Thee, turn to Thee;
At last, I, homeward turning,
    Come to Thee.

H. LL J.

( 53 )

# Edeyrn. 7.6. D.

Alaw Gymreig.
Cynghaneddwyd gan W. J. H.

( 54 )

TEILWNG yw 'r Oen a laddwyd,
  O'r holl ogoniant mawr,
Trwy ganol nef y nefoedd,
  Ac yma ar y llawr ;
Pan elo 'r holl greadigaeth
  Yn ulw gan y tân,
Teilyngdod Iesu drosof,
  Fydd fy nhragwyddol gân.

2 Agorodd ddrws i'r caethion,
  I ddod o'r cystudd mawr ;
A'i werthfawr waed fe dalodd
  Eu dyled oll i lawr :
Nid oes dim damnedigaeth
  I neb o'r duwiol had—
Y gwaredigion canant
  Am rinwedd mawr Ei waed.

MORGAN RHYS.

1 I NEED Thee, precious Jesus,
  I need a friend like Thee,
A friend to soothe and pity,
  A friend to care for me.
I need the heart of Jesus
  To feel each anxious care,
To tell my every trouble,
  And all my sorrows share.

2 I need Thee, precious Jesus,
  And hope to see Thee soon,
Encircled with the rainbow
  And seated on Thy throne :
There, with Thy blood-bought children,
  My joy shall ever be
To sing Thy praises, Jesus,
  To gaze, my Lord, on Thee.

E

# Edifeiriol. M.H.

O " Caniadau y Cyssegr."

PECHADUR wyf, da gwyr fy Nuw,
  Llawn o archollion o bob rhyw ;
Yn byw mewn eisieu o waed y groes,
Bob mynyd awr o'r dydd a'r nos.

WILLIAMS.

O ! ARGLWYDD, cofia 'th angau drud,
  A'th boenau mawrion yn y byd !
A dadleu rhai'n, ag uchel lef,
Tros f'enaid tlawd yn nghanol nef.

WILLIAMS.

1 OH ! come, and mourn with me awhile,
    Oh ! come ye to the Saviour's side ;
  Oh ! come, together let us mourn,
    Jesus, our Love, is crucified

2 Come, take thy stand beneath the cross ;
    And let the blood from out His side
  Fall gently on thee drop by drop ;
    Jesus, our Love, is crucified.

3 Oh ! love of God, Oh ! sin of man,
    In this dread act your strength is tried ;
  And victory remains with love ;
    For He, our Love, is crucified,

FABER.

# Edinburgh. 8.7.D.

Alaw Gymreig.   Y cynghaneddiad gan mwyaf gan
y Parch SYR F. A. G. OUSELEY, Barwnig, M.A., Mus. Doc.

1 DYFAIS fawr tragwyddol gariad,
    Ydyw iachawdwriaeth lawn ;
Sail cyfammod hedd sydd gadarn,
    Ac nis derfydd byth mo'i ddawn :
Dyma 'r man y gorphwys f' enaid,
    Dyma 'r man y byddaf byw,
Mewn tangnefedd pur, heddychol,
    Yn mhob 'stormydd gyda'm Duw.

2 Syfled iechyd, syfled bywyd,
    Cnawd a chalon yn gytûn ;
Byth ni syfla ammod heddwch—
    Hen gytundeb TRI YN UN :
Dianwadal yw 'r addewid,
    Cadarn byth yw cynghor Duw :
Cysur cryf i'r neb a gredo 'n
    Haeddiant Iesu i gael byw.

                                T. CHARLES.


### PSALM CXLVIII.

1 PRAISE the Lord, ye heavens adore Him ;
    Praise Him, angels in the height ;
Sun and moon, rejoice before Him ;
    Praise Him, all ye stars of light :
Praise the Lord, for He hath spoken ;
    Worlds His mighty voice obeyed :
Laws that never shall be broken,
    For their guidance He hath made.

2 Praise the Lord, for He is glorious ;
    Never shall His promise fail :
God hath made His saints victorious ;
    Sin and death shall not prevail :
Praise the God of our salvation,
    Hosts on high, His power proclaim ;
Heaven and earth, and all creation,
    Laud and magnify His name.

                                MANT.

# Elwy. 8.7.D.

Alaw Gymreig, wedi ei chynghaneddu
gan W. J. H.

FINE.

D.C.

( 60 )

1 NEFOL Dad, Dy fendith anfon,
   Ar Dy blant sydd yma ynghyd;
Gosod ni ar fynydd Seion,
   Llanw, dena ein holl fryd:
Dysg ni roi i'th enw wiw-glod,
   Dysg ni gadw'th ddeddfau glan,
Dyro ffydd, a lyno ynod
   Yn y dwr, ac yn y tan.

2 O! Iachawdwr, fuost unwaith
   Blentyn bychan fel nyni,
·Gwylia'n camrau, nodda'n llesgedd,
   Gwna ni'n debyg iawn i Ti:
Dwg Dy wyn pan fônt flinderus,
   Yn Dy freichiau, ar Dy fron,
Trwy yr anial fyd galarus,
   I'r orphwysfa nefol lon.

3 Santaidd Ysbryd, taena'th edyn,
   Euraidd, canaid, tros ein pen;
Arwain ni, a dysg in' ddilyn
   Llwybrau hedd i'r nefoedd wen;
Trigo wnelot yn ein calon,
   A'n haddasu tra bôm byw,
I etifeddu gwlad y goron,
   Gwlad ein Hiesu, gwlad ein Duw.

*Cyf. gan* A. R.


HEAVENLY Father, send Thy blessing
   On Thy children gathered here;
May they all, Thy name confessing,
   Be to Thee for ever dear:
May they be, like Joseph, loving,
   Dutiful, and chaste, and pure;
And their faith, like David, proving
   Steadfast unto death, endure.

( 61 )

## Hyfrydol. 8.7. D.

R. H. Pritchard.
Cynghaneddwyd gan W. J. H.

( 62 )

BETH yw'r udgorn glywa'i'n seinio'?
  Brenin Seilo sydd yn gwa'dd :
Pwy sy'n cael eu galw ganddo ?
  Pechaduriaid o bob gradd :
Adre', adre', blant afradlawn,
  Gadewch gibau gweigion ffôl ;
Clywaf lais y Brenin heddyw
  'N para i alw ar eich ôl.

R. PHILLIPS.

CADBEN mawr ein hiachawdwriaeth,
  Welaf yn y frwydr hon ;
Holl elynion Ei ddyweddi
  Yn gorfod plygu ger Ei fron :
Plant afradlawn sy'n dod adref,
  A fu 'mhell o dir eu gwlad ;
Rhai fu'n fudion sy'n clodfori
  Duw am iachawdwriaeth rad.

MORGAN RHYS.

1 COME, Thou long expected Jesus,
    Born to set Thy people free ;
From our fears and sins release us,
    Let us find our rest in Thee :
Israel's strength and consolation,
    Hope of all the earth Thou art ;
Dear desire of every nation,
    Joy of every longing heart.

2 Born Thy people to deliver ;
    Born a Child, and yet a King ;
Born to reign in us for ever,
    Now Thy gracious kingdom bring :
By Thine own eternal Spirit,
    Rule in all our hearts alone ;
By Thine all-sufficient merit,
    Raise us to Thy glorious throne.

MADAN,

# Melai. 8.7.4.

W. H. R., 1875.

( 64 )

1 GWEL uwchlaw cymylau amser,
     O ! fy enaid, gwel y tir,
 Lle mae'r awel fyth yn dyner
     Lle mae'r wybren fyth yn glir !
         Hapus dyrfa,
     Sydd yn nofio yn ei hedd !

2 Nid oes yno neb yn wylo,
     Nid·oes yno neb yn brudd,
 Troir yn fêl y wermod yno,
     Yno rhoir y caeth yn rhydd ;
         Hapus dyrfa,
     Sydd a'u trigfa yno mwy !

3 Mae fy nghalon brudd yn llamu
     O orfoledd dan fy mron,
 Yn y gobaith am feddianu
     'Retifeddiaeth ddwyfol hon :
         Hapus dyrfa,
     Sydd a'u hwyneb tua'r wlad !

                              ISLWYN.


1 GUIDE me, O Thou great Jehovah !
     Pilgrim through this barren land ;
 I·am weak, but Thou art mighty—
     Hold me with Thy powerful hand :
         Bread of heaven,
     Feed me till I want no more.

2 When I tread the verge of Jordan,
     Bid my anxious fears subside ;
 Bear me through the swelling torrent,
     Land me safe on Canaan's side :
         Songs of praises,
     I will ever give to Thee.

                              WILLIAMS.

# Pembroke. 6.8.4.

Sylfaenedig ar Alaw Gymreig.
Cynghaneddwyd gan W. J. H.

1 AM fod fy Iesu 'n fyw,
　　Byw hefyd fydd Ei saint ;
Er gorfod goddef poen a briw,
　　Mawr yw eu braint :
Bydd melus lanio draw,
　　'Nol bod o don i don ;
Ac mi ro'f ffarwel yn Dy law,
　　I'r ddaear hon.

2 O ! angau pur y groes,
　　Ti bellach fydd fy nghân,
'Doedd dwfr i'w gael ond ar y groes,
　　A'm golchai'n lân :
Y ffynnon loyw lawn,
　　Sydd barod iawn o hyd,
I olchi'r Ethiop du yn wyn,
　　Hyd eithaf byd.

J. THOMAS.


1 THE God of Abraham praise,
　　Who reigns enthroned above,
Ancient of everlasting days,
　　And God of love !
Jehovah ! great I AM !
　　By earth and heaven confest ;
I bow and bless the sacred name,
　　For ever blest.

2 He by Himself hath sworn,
　　I on His oath depend ;
I shall, on eagle' wings upborne
　　To heaven ascend ;
I shall behold His face,
　　I shall His power adore,
And sing the wonders of His grace
　　For evermore.

OLIVER.

( 67 )

# Sannan. 8.7. D.

Alaw Gymreig. Cynghaneddwyd gan
y diweddar Barch. J. B. DYKES, M.A., Mus. Doc.

M I edrychaf ar i fyny,
Deued tywyllwch, deued nos;
Os daw heddwch im' o unlle,
Daw o haeddiant gwaed y groes:
Dyna'r man y gwnaf fy nhrigfan,
Dyna'r man gobeithiaf mwy;
Nid oes iechyd fyth i'm henaid,
Ond mewn dwyfol farwol glwy'.

WILLIAMS.


1 SEE the King desired for ages,
By the just expected long;
Long implored, at length He hasteth,
Cometh with salvation strong:
Oh! how past all utterance happy,
Sweet and joyful will it be,
When they who, unseen, have loved Him,
Jesus face to face shall see!

2 What will be the bliss and rapture
None can dream and none can tell,
There to reign among the angels,
In that heavenly home to dwell!
To those realms, O Saviour, call me;
Deign to open that blest gate;
Thou whom, seeking, looking, longing,
I, with eager hope, await!

*Trans. by* MRS. CHARLES.

( 69 )

# SUBSCRIBERS.

Argent, W. I., Esq., Birkenhead
Arlett, Mr. Charles, Seacombe
Arthur, Mr. J. Beynon, Carmarthen
Asaph, The Right Rev. the Lord Bishop of St.

Bangor, The Right Rev. the Lord Bishop of
Bangor, The Very Rev. the Dean of
Brereton, A. J., Esq. (Andreas o Vôn), Mold
 (4 copies)
Byrth, Rev. Stewart, M.A., Seacombe

Casson, Thomas, Esq., Denbigh
Chalmers, F., Esq., Lancaster Gate, London
Chambres, P. H., Esq., J. P., Llysmeirchion,
 Denbighshire
Chambres, William, Esq., J. P., Dolben, St.
 Asaph (2 copies)
Charles, Rev. David, D.D., Aberdyfi
Charles, D. R., E q., Ulverston (6 copies)
Collett, M. W., Esq., Sussex Square, London
Croft, Mr. William, Victoria St., Liverpool

Daniel, Mr. John, Henllan
Daniels, Mr. Daniel, Liverpool
Davies, Mr. Abel, Upper Beau St., Liverpool
Davies, Mr. David, New Brighton
Davies, Rev. David, Henllan
Davies, Rev. David Charles, D.D., London
Davies, Mr. D. E., North Parade, Aber-
 ystwyth
Davies, Mr. D. H., Bootle
Davies, Mr. Edward, Claughton
Davies, Mr. Edward, Henllan
Davies, Mr. Edward, Rock Ferry
Davies, Ellis, Esq., Liscard
Davies, Mr. Evan R., Birkenhead
Davies, Mr. Hugh, Llanfair, Welshpool
Davies, Mr. Ioan T., Pensarn, Abergele
Davies, Mr. Isaac (Nabl), Trefnant

Davies, Mr. Jacob, Liverpool
Davies, Mr. John, Broughton, Manchester
 (2 copies)
Davies, Mr. John, Seacombe
Davies, Mr. John Edward, Bootle
Davies, Mr. J. J., Denbigh
Davies, Mr. Joseph, Birkenhead
Davies, Mr. Morris, Upper Bangor
Davies, Richard, Esq., M.P., Treborth Hall,
 Carnarvonshire
Davies, Mr. R. G., Denbigh
Davies, Mr. R. O., Pickering Terrace,
 London
Davies, Mr. Thomas, London Rd., London
Davies, Mr. William, Denbigh
Davies, Mr. William, Bryn Parc, Henllan
Davies, William, Esq. (Mynorydd), London
Davies, Mr. Wm., Penfforddwen, Nantglyn
Davydd, Mr. Gwilym, Liverpool
Drury, Mr. Robert, Liverpool

Earle, Mr. T. Bolton, Birkenhead
Edwards, Mrs., St. Domingo Grove, Liverpool
Edwards, Rev. Ellis, M.A., Bala (2 copies)
Edwards, Mr. Evan, Caeffynon, Aberystwyth
 (2 copies)
Edwards, Mr. Hugh, Carlton Road, London
Edwards, Mr. John, Egremont
Edwards, Mr. John, Belford Street South,
 Liverpool
Edwards, Mr. Peter, Barrow-in-Furness
Edwards, Rev. T. C., M.A., Principal of Uni-
 versity College, Aberystwyth
Edwards, T. Gold, Esq., Denbigh
Ellis, Mr. Edward, Denbigh
Ellis, Rev. Griffith, B.A., Bootle
Ellis, Mr. John, Seacombe
Ellis, Mr. Robert, Manchester (2 copies)
Enyon, Mr. R. C., Bootle (2 copies)

# SUBSCRIBERS.

Evans, A. P., Esq., Anfield
Evans, Rev. D. Charles, Rhyl
Evans, Mr. Edward, Henllan
Evans, Mr. Elias, Birkenhead (4 *copies*)
Evans, Rev. Ellis W., M.A., Colwyn
Evans, Rev. Emrys, Cotton Hall, Denbigh
Evans, Mr. E., Alt Street, Liverpool
Evans, Mr. Evan, Henblas, Nantglyn
Evans, Mr. Evan, Seacombe
Evans, Mr. John (Ab Owen), Cardiff
Evans, Mr. John, Llanfair, Welshpool
Evans, Mr. John, Seacombe
Evans, Mr. Joseph, Henllan
Evans, Mr. O. M. F., Liverpool
Evans, Mr. R. C., Tynewydd, Llanfairfechan
Evans, Stephen, Esq., London (4 *copies*)
Evans, Mr. Thos., Exmouth St., Birkenhead
Evans, Thomas, Esq., Prospect Vale, Fairfield
Evans, Mr. Thomas, New Brighton
Evans, William, Esq., Holywell
Evans, Wm., Jun., Esq., Bootle (2 *copies*)
Evans, Mr. Wm., Ty Crwn, Henllan (3 *copies*)
Evans, Mr. William, Conyers St., Liverpool

Foulkes, Mr. Abel, Liverpool
Foulkes, Mr. Isaac, Liverpool
Foulkes, Rev. John, Ruthin
Foulkes, Mr. W. T., Llechryd, Llannefydd
Frimston, Mr. John, Liverpool

Gee, E. W., Esq., Whitchurch, Denbigh
Gee, Robert, Esq., M.D., Liverpool
Gee, Thomas, Esq., Denbigh
Gee, Thomas, Esq., Liverpool
Gibson, Mr. R. Ll., Liverpool
Gray, Rev. Thomas, Rhyl
Green, Mr. R. J., North Bank, London
Griffith, David, Esq., Bron Eyarth, Ruthin
Griffith, Mr. Ebenezer, Henllan
Griffith, John, Esq., Egremont (4 *copies*)
Griffith, Mr. Robert, Henllan
Griffiths, Mr. Edward, Regent Rd., Liverpool
Griffiths, Mr. John, Norfolk Terrace, London
Griffiths, Rev. John, D.D., Vicar of Llandeilo, and Proctor for St. David's
Griffiths, Mr. Robert, Henllan
Griffiths, Mr. Thomas, Egremont

Hamilton, F. A., Esq., Brent Lodge, Finchley, near London
Hastings, Mr. T. E., Marsh Lane, Linacre
Heaton, J. R., Esq., Plas Heaton, Denbighshire (4 *copies*)
Heriot, J. H., Esq., Ullet Road, Liverpool (2 *copies*)
Hill, Mr. F. A., Wood Green, near London
Hoskier, H., Esq., Solna, Roehampton, near London
Howell, Rev. David, The Vicarage, Wrexham
Hughes, David, Esq., St. Domingo Grove, Liverpool
Hughes, Mr. Edwd., Heywood St., Manchester
Hughes, Mr. Elias, Peniel, near Denbigh
Hughes, Mr. Hugh, Whetstone Lane, Tranmere
Hughes, Mr. Hugh, Conyers Street, Liverpool
Hughes, Mr. H. O., Bangor
Hughes, H. R., Esq., Kinmel, Kinmel Park, Abergele (4 *copies*)
Hughes, Miss Jane G., The Palace, St. Asaph
Hughes, Mr. John, Henllan
Hughes, Rev. John, Liverpool
Hughes, John, Esq., Rock Mount, Prince's Park, Liverpool
Hughes, Mr. John, Rock Ferry
Hughes, Mr. J. H., Plas Chambres, Denbigh
Hughes, J. R., Esq., St. Domingo Grove, Liverpool
Hughes, Mr. Lot, Hemans Street, Liverpool
Hughes, Mr. Owen, Premier Street, Liverpool
Hughes, Mr. Richard, Fronhill St., Liverpool
Hughes, Mr. Robert, Heywood St., Manchester
Hughes, Mr. R. E., Whetsone Lane, Tranmere
Hughes, Mr. Thos., Stonewall Street, Liverpool
Hughes, Mr. Thomas, Pendre, Llanfyllin
Hughes, Mr. T. O., Liverpool
Hughes, Mr. T. P., Vale Street, Denbigh (2 *copies*)
Hughes, Rev. Wm., Groes, Henllan (5 *copies*)
Hughes, Mr. Wm., Lodge Lane, Liverpool
Hughes, Mr. Wm., Norfolk Terrace, London
Hughes, Mr. Wm., Yale Villas, Walton
Humphreys, Mr. Calwaladr, Llanfair, Welshpool

Humphreys, Mr. Owen, New Brighton
Humphreys, Mr. Wm., Bootle

JENKINS, Rev. John, M.A., Connah's Quay (2 copies)
Jones, Mrs., Post Office, Nantglyn
Jones, Mr. Arthur W. J. Skeinner, Plashen, Anglesea
Jones, Rev. Benjamin, Bagillt
Jones, Rev. D., Vicar of Dyserth
Jones, Mr. David, Aubrey Street, Liverpool
Jones, Mr. David, Waterloo Terrace, London
Jones, Mr. David, Somerville, Seacombe (2 copies)
Jones, Mr. Ebenezer, Birkenhead
Jones, Mr. Edward, Llanllechid
Jones, Mr. Edward, Price St., Birkenhead
Jones, Edward, Esq., Church St., Egremont
Jones, Mr. Edward, Jun., Church Street, Egremont
Jones, Mr. Edward, White Rock Street, Liverpool
Jones, Mr. Edward, Pwllheli
Jones, Mr. E. Garmon, Liverpool
Jones, Mr. E., Borth, near Aberystwyth
Jones, Mr. Evan, Tue Brook, Liverpool
Jones, Mr. Griffith, Bootle
Jones, Mr. H., Foxhill Street, Liverpool
Jones, Rev. Hugh, Liverpool
Jones, Mr. H. Ll., Somerville, Seacombe (2 copies)
Jones, Rev. Isaac, Glan'rafon, Wrexham
Jones, Mr. James, Henllan
Jones, Mr. John, N. and S.W. Bank, Birkenhead
Jones, Mr. John, Wellington Rd., Egremont
Jones, Mr. John, Lombard Street, Liverpool
Jones, Mr. John, North Bank, London
Jones, Mr. John, Berain, Llannefydd
Jones, Mr. John, Shaw Street, Seacombe
Jones, Mr. John, St. Asaph
Jones, Mr. J. E. Church Street, Egremont
Jones, Mr. J. E., South Hunter St., Liverpool
Jones, Mr. J. E., Harland Road, Tranmere
Jones, Mr. J. H., Thackeray Street, Liverpool
Jones, Mr. J. R., Stalmine Road, Walton
Jones, Rev. Jonathan, Tywyn, Abergele

Jones, Mr. Joseph, St. Andrew St., Manchester
Jones, Miss Mary, Henllan
Jones, Rev. Michael, Flint
Jones, Mr. Moses, Llannefydd
Jones, Mr. Owen, Price Street, Birkenhead
Jones, Mr. Owen, Henllan
Jones, Rev. Owen, B.A., Liverpool (2 copies)
Jones, Rev. Owen, B.A., Newtown, (2 copies)
Jones, Rev. Owen, Pentrevoelas (2 copies)
Jones, Mr. Owen, Plas Gwyn, Pwllheli
Jones, Rev. Peter, Birkenhead
Jones, Rev. P. W., Penygroes, Carnarvonshire
Jones, Mr. Richard, Aubrey Street, Liverpool
Jones, Mr. R., Abergele
Jones, Mr. Robert, Henllan
Jones, Mr. Robert, New Brighton
Jones, Rev. R. A., Abergele
Jones, Mr. R. H., Llansannan
Jones, Mr. R. P., Tunnel Road, Liverpool
Jones, Mr. R. S., Egremont (2 copies)
Jones, Mr. Samuel (Ap Cunllo), Llangeler
Jones, Mr. S. Allen, Mold
Jones, Mr. Thomas, Barton St., Birkenhead
Jones, Mr. Thomas Ll., Edinburgh (2 copies)
Jones, Mr. Thomas, Cwm, Henllan
Jones, Mr. Thomas, Henllan
Jones, Mr. Thomas, Everton Road, Liverpool
Jones, Wm., Esq., M.D., Plashen, Anglesea
Jones, Mr. William, Denbigh Street, Henllan
Jones, Mr. William, Henllan
Jones, Mr. William, Elstow Street, Liverpool
Jones, Mr. William, Everton Brow, Liverpool
Jones, William, Esq., Rock Ferry
Jones, W. H., Esq., Church Street, Egremont
Jones, Mr. W. J., Ystradgynlais
Jones, Mr. W. O., Llanfachreth

KNOWLES, Robt., Esq., Beech Rd., Tranmere

LEE, Mr. Frederick, Miles Street, Liverpool
Lewis, Miss, Caerwys
Lewis, Mr. David, Hope Street, Liverpool
Lewis, Mr. David, Llanrhystyd
Lewis, Enoch, Esq., Mostyn (3 copies)
Lewis, Hugh, Esq., Liverpool (2 copies)
Lewis, Mr. John, Athol Street, Liverpool
Lewis, Mr. Owen, Mornington Crescent, London

Lewis, Rev. Robert, Carnarvon
Lloyd, Miss, Abergele
Lloyd, Mrs., Magazine Park, New Brighton
Lloyd, Mr. Edward, jun., Abergele
Lloyd, Mr. John, Felin Segrwyd, Henllan
Lloyd, Mr. John, Richmond Terrace, Liverpool (4 copies)
Lloyd, Mr. John Ambrose, Chester
Lloyd, Mr. John Henry, Butler St., Manchester
Lloyd, Thomas, Esq., Magazine Park, New Brighton
Lumley, Mr. G. E., Egremont
Lumley, Rev. Richard, Egremont
Lumley, Mr. Richard, Egremont
Lumley, Mr. Richard, Liverpool

MACHEN, M. S., Esq., Tranmere
Mainwaring, Charles Salusbury, Esq., Galltfaenan, Denbighshire
Mainwaring, Townshend, Esq., Galltfaenan, Denbighshire (2 copies)
Marks, Mr. Richard, Birkenhead
Matthews, Rev. Edward, Cardiff
Matthews, Mr. H., Seacombe
McGaul, Mr. J. H., Tranmere
Miles, G. E., Esq., M.R.C.S., Denbigh
Mills, Mr. Edward, Denbigh
Mills, James, Esq., Falkner Street, Liverpool (2 copies)
Morgan, Mr. David, Plan Street, Liverpool
Morgan, Mr. Evan, Great Dark Gate Street, Aberystwyth
Morgan, Mr. H., Tavistock Place, London
Morgan, Mr. M. Fairleigh Road, London
Morris, Mr. D. Jones, Lleweni Hall, Denbigh
Morris, Mr. John, Cefn Berain, Llannefydd
Morris, Mr. Robert, Ffynon Ddu, Gytfylliog
Morris, Mr. W., Morland Street, Liverpool
Morton, Rev. W., St. Asaph
Moyes, Mr. Thomas, Denbigh

NEWTON, Mr. G. A., Field Street, Liverpool
Nicholas, Rev. W. Ll., B.A., Rhyl

OLIVER, Mr. J. R., Seacombe
Owen, David E., Esq., Church St., Egremont
Owen, Rev. Daniel, Mold (2 copies)

Owen, Edward, Esq., Rock Ferry
Owen, Mr. Jeremiah, Gillar Street, Merthyr Tydfil
Owen, Hugh, Esq., London (2 copies)
Owen, John, Esq. (Owain Alaw), Chester
Owen, Rev. John, M.A., Criccieth
Owen, John, Esq., Egremont (3 copies)
Owen, Mr. J. G., Church Street, Liverpool
Owen, Mr. Owen G., Seldon Street, Liverpool
Owen, Rev. Robert, Gwaenynog Farm, Denbigh
Owen, Rev. R. Llugwy, Acrfair, Ruabon
Owen, Mr. T., Lowther Street, Liverpool
Owen, Mr. Thomas, Queen's Rd., Liverpool
Owen, Mr. T. R., Price Street, Birkenhead
Owen, Mr. Wm., Jun., Sarn, near Pwllheli
Owens, Mr. John, Tower View, Seacombe
Owens, Rev. Owen, Liverpool
Owens, Mr. Owen, Spencer Steeet, Liverpool
Owens, Mr. Robert, Tower View, Seacombe

PARRY, Miss, York St., Cheetham, Manchester
Parry, Mr. E. R., Pool Road, Egremont
Parry, Rev. Griffith, Manchester
Parry, Joseph, Esq., Mus. Bac., University College, Aberystwyth
Parry, Mr. Joseph, St. Domingo Grove, Liverpool
Parry, Mr. William, Birkenhead
Peters, Mr. John, Maesywaen, Bala
Peters, Edward, Esq., Chester (6 copies)
Pierce, Evan, Esq., M.D., Denbigh (4 copies)
Pierce, Mr. John, Birkenhead
Pooley, Frederick, Esq., Egremont
Powell, Mr. Benjamin, Mold
Powell, Rev. Ebenezer, Chester
Powell, Mr. R. J., Myrtle Street, Liverpool
Pritchard, Mr. Evan, Stoneycroft, Liverpool
Pritchard, Mr. John B., Brynwoodjohn, Henllan
Pritchard, Mr. Joseph, Orlando Street, Bootle
Pritchard, Mr. Thomas, Bedford Road, Rock Ferry
Pugh, Eliezer, Esq., Falkner Street, Liverpool
Pugh, Mr. Howel (Hywel ap Huw), Birkenhead
Pugh, J. H., Esq., Elm Grove, Tranmere

Pugh, Mr. J. L., Brunswick Street, Liverpool (2 *copies*)

Pughe, Mr. R., Tanyglog, Llanfair, Welshpool

RANDLES, Mr. Charles, Newlands St., Liverpool

Randles, Mr. Thomas, Everton Village, Liverpool

Rees, Ebenezer, Esq., Liverpool (2 *copies*)

Rees, Mr. John, Suffolk Street, London

Rees, Mr. Rees, University College, Aberystwyth

Rees, Mr. Samuel, Grey Rock St., Liverpool

Rees, Mr. Thomas, Gillar St., Merthyr Tydfil

Rhys, John, Esq., M.A., formerly Fellow of Merton College, Oxford

Richard, Henry, Esq., M.P., London

Richards, Brinley, Esq., London

Richards, Mr. James, Hampstead, nr. London

Richards, W. H., Esq., Mellor's Buildings, Liverpool

Roberts, Mrs., Plas Harri, Llannefydd

Roberts, Rev. Aaron, M.A., Vicar of Newchurch, Carmarthen (2 *copies*)

Roberts, Mr. Arthur, Henllan

Roberts, David, Esq., Tanyrallt, Abergele (6 *copies*)

Roberts, Mr. Edward, Temperance Hotel, Denbigh

Roberts, Mr. E., Penarth, Llanfair, Welshpool

Roberts, Mr. Eleazer, Liverpool

Roberts, Mr. Griffith, St. John's Road, Liverpool

Roberts, Mr. Jesse, Rochdale Road, Manchester

Roberts, John, Esq., J.P., Bryngwenallt, Abergele (6 *copies*)

Roberts, Rev. John, Edinburgh (4 *copies*)

Roberts, Mr. John, Foxhall, Henllan (2 *copies*)

Roberts, Mr. John, Glasmor, Nantglyn (2 *copies*)

Roberts, Mr. John, Well House, Saltney

Roberts, Mr. J. ap E., Y Ddôl, Llannefydd

Roberts, Rev. J. J., Trefriw

Roberts, Mr. Lewis, Compton Road, London

Roberts, Mr. Meshach, Bangor

Roberts, Mr. Peter, St. Asaph (2 *copies*)

Roberts, Mr. P. Lewis, Denbigh

Roberts, Richard, Esq., Mossley Hill, Aigburth (2 *copies*)

Roberts, Mr. Robert, Brynffanigl, Abergele

Roberts, Mr. Robert, Penypalmant, Denbigh

Roberts, Mr. Robt., Tanrhiw, Groes, Henllan

Roberts, Mr. Robert, Burleigh Road South, Liverpool

Roberts, Mr. R. (Eos Brynllwyd) Llannefydd

Roberts, Mr. Robert, Trefnant (4 *copies*)

Roberts, Rev. Thomas, Bethesda, Bangor

Roberts, Mr. Thos., Penybontfawr, Oswestry

Roberts, Mr. William, Llwydfaen, Conway

Roberts, William, Esq., Catharine Street, Liverpool

Roberts, Mr. William, Lonsdale St., Liverpool

Roberts, Mr. William, Llannefydd

Robinson, Mr. John, Denbigh

Rogers, Mr. Edward, Peniel, Denbigh

Rogers, Thomas Esq., Beach Bank, Liscard

SALISBURY, E. G., Esq., Chester

Salisbury, Mr. John, Henllan

Salisbury, Mr. Robt., Waen-dwysog, Henllan

Samuel, Mr. Thomas, Aberystwyth

Saunders, Rev. David, Swansea

Sayce, Rev. A. H., M.A., Fellow and Tutor of Queen's College, Cambridge

Seager, C. L., Esq., Palace Hotel, Southport

Simner, Abel, Esq., London

Smart, Rev. Edward, M.A., The Rectory, Henllan (4 *copies*)

Story, Mr. David, Penparcllwyd, Henllan (2 *copies*)

Story, Mr. William, Llanfair, Welshpool (3 *copies*)

Story, Mr. John, Henllan

THEODORE, Mr. Wm., Llanfair, Welshpool

Thomas, Mr. B. J., Northumberland Terrace, Liverpool

Thomas, Mr. D., West Terrace, Chester

Thomas, Rev. Edward, Llanfair Talhaiarn

Thomas, Rev. Edward, New Brighton

Thomas, Evan, Esq., Bryneglwys, Anglesea (2 *copies*)

Thomas, Mr. John, Alwyn Villas, London
Thomas, Mr. John, New Brighton (2 *copies*)
Thomas, Rev. J., Rhyl
Thomas, Mr. Josiah, Heathville, Tranmere
Thomas, Mr. R., Bontnewydd
Thomas, Mr. W., Bontnewydd
Thomas, Rev. Robert, Garston
Thomas, Mr. Robert, Scotland Rd., Liverpool
Thomas, Rev. Robert, Llanllyfni
Thomas, Mr. R. J., Hunt Street, Liverpool
Thomas, Mr. Thomas, Market Place South, Birkenhead
Thompson, Mr. James, Birkenhead
Thraves, Mr. Edwin, Tranmere
Tilley, H. A., Esq., F.R.G.S., London

Vaughan, Mr. Edward, Berain, Llannefydd
Vaughan, Mr. John, Penybryn, Abergele
Vaughan, Mr. John, Mardy Estate, Merthyr Tydfil
Venmore, Mr. James, Venmore St., Liverpool

Washington, Mr. Daniel, Liverpool
Watkins, Mr. D. R., London
West, W. Cornwallis, Esq., Ruthin Castle, Denbighshire (2 *copies*)
Williams, Mr. Abel, Liverpool
Williams, Mr. B. M., Denbigh
Williams, Mr. Cadwaladr, Seacombe
Williams, Mr. David, Bangor
Williams, Mr. D. Parry, Denbigh
Williams, Mr. Ebenezer, Bradford Street, Manchester
Williams, Mr. E. E. (Nefydd Ddu) St. George (3 *copies*)
Williams, Mr. Griffith, York Terrace, Liverpool
Williams, Mr. Henry, Plas Uchaf, Llannefydd
Williams, Rev. James, Chester
Williams, Mr. John, Foel, near Denbigh
Williams, John, Esq., Great Mersey Street, Liverpool (8 *copies*)

Williams, Rev. John, Talybon
Williams, Mr. J. D., Henllan
Williams, Mr. J. E., Abergele
Williams, Mr. J. H., Henllan
Williams, Mr. J. J., Noel Street, Liverpool
Williams, Mr. Lloyd, Collyhurst, Manchester
Williams, Rev. Morris, Denbigh
Williams, Mr. Owen, Glanclwyd, Bodfari
Williams. Mr. Peter, Liverpool
Williams, Mr. Pierce, Garnedd Uchaf, near Denbigh
Williams, Mr. Richard, Post-Office, Dolgelley
Williams, Mr. Robert, Rock Ferry (6 *copies*)
Williams, Mr. R. Howarth, Nantclwyd House, Ruthin
Williams, Mr. Samuel, Rutland St., Liverpool
Williams, Thomas, Esq., Hamilton Square, Birkenhead
Williams, Mr. Thomas, Vale Street, Denbigh
Williams, Mr. Thomas, Pimblet Street, Manchester
Williams, Mr. Thomas, Stocks Street, Manchester
Williams, T. J., Esq., Mayor of Denbigh
Williams, T. M., Esq., London
Williams, Watkin, Esq., Q.C., M.P., Plas Draw, Ruthin
Williams, W., Esq, M.B., Medical Superintendent of N.W. Asylum, Denbigh
Williams, Mr. W., Parc Canol, Denbigh
Williams, Mr. W., St. George's Hill, Liverpool
Williams, Mr. W., Whitefield Road, Liverpool
Williams, Mr. William, Jun., Llannefydd
Williams, Mr. William, New Brighton
Williams, W. H., Esq, Moss Bank, Liverpool
Williams, W. Maysmor, Esq., Chester
Williams, Rev. W. O., F.R.A.S., Liverpool
Williams, Rev. W.P., London
Wynne, Mr. William, Walton

Young, J. D., Esq., Glasgow.

Lightning Source UK Ltd.
Milton Keynes UK
UKHW030902240119
336116UK00007B/111/P